Shutterbug Books
SCIENCE

Matter All Around

by Thea Franklin

STECK-VAUGHN
Harcourt Supplemental Publishers

www.steck-vaughn.com

Contents

What Is Matter?

Look around you! What do you see?

You may see mountains and trees, or deep blue water.

What do all these things have in common?

They are all forms of matter!

SOLIDS

All things are made of matter.

There are different forms, or kinds, of matter.

One form of matter is a **SOLID**.

Most of the objects you see are solids.
Desks and chairs are solids.
The floor and the walls are solids, too.

Look outside.

What solids do you see?

The park bench and the sidewalk are solids.

Rocks and mountains are solids, too.
A solid has a shape of its own.
A solid cannot easily change shape.

Liquids

Liquid is another form of matter.
Liquid can move and flow.
Liquid can easily change shape.

Water is a liquid.

You can pour water into a fishbowl.

The water takes the shape of the fishbowl.

Look around you.
What other liquids do you see?
Raindrops are liquid.

Rivers and lakes are liquids.
Waterfalls are liquids, too.
The ocean is made of a lot of liquid!

Gases

Another form of matter is **gas**.
Gases are all around you.
The air you breathe is a gas.

Hot air balloons are filled with gas.
The gas makes the balloons float in the air.
Without the gas, they would lie flat on the ground.

Some signs use another kind of gas.
Glass tubes are filled with this gas.
The gas makes the light tubes glow!

Look closely at this picture.
What **SOLIDS**, *Liquids*, and **Gases**
can you find?

Matter can be a solid, liquid, or gas.
Matter is all around you.
Even you are made of matter!